MICROWAVE BOTTLING FRUIT, JAMS, JELLIES Pickles & Sauces

Isabel Webb

The Five Mile Press

The Five Mile Press
379 Smith Street
Fitzroy Victoria 3065 Australia

First published 1989

Reprinted with corrections 1990

Copyright © Isabel Webb

Design by Geoff Hocking

Illustrations © The Five Mile Press
Illustrations by Bronwyn Traill
Photography by Neil Lorimer

Typeset by Bookset Pty Ltd, Melbourne
Printed in Singapore by Kyodo Printing Co Ltd

National Library of Australia Cataloguing-in-Publication Data

Webb, Isabel, 1936–
Microwave bottling fruit, jams, jellies, pickles and sauces.

Includes index.
ISBN 0 86788 138 0.

1. Food – Preservation. 2. Microwave cookery. I. Title.

641.4'2

Contents

1

Introduction

For many people, fruit-bottling conjures up nostalgic visions of a typical country kitchen overflowing with seasonal fruits waiting to be bottled — a task that involves many hours of work. But the days of bulky, expensive and complex equipment are gone. Now, anyone with a microwave oven can prepare the delicious and nutritious preserves, jams and pickles that were a prized feature of our grandparents' larders. And, most importantly, the microwave method enables you to preserve the harvest of a single backyard tree, or take advantage of bumper commercial crops.

When bottling and preserving in a microwave oven, the finished products are closer to their natural form, they retain their nutritious value and boast enhanced colour, shape and flavour. After years of experimenting with bottling methods in my microwave I continue to be astonished at the excellent results.

For me, the microwave bottling method has revolutionised the preserving of fruit, jams, jellies, chutneys and pickles. If you follow carefully the directions and recipes in this book you will rediscover the immense pleasures of beautiful bottled preserves.

The Microwave Oven

Don't be concerned about placing metal objects in your microwave oven. The small ratio of metal compound to the other substances involved in the bottling process will not cause any arcing or damage to the oven. As a precaution, always allow a space of at least 3 centimetres (1¼ inches) between jars and the oven wall.

The cooking times given in this book are for a 650-watt microwave. For a microwave of 500–550-watt capacity, allow one extra minute of cooking time for every additional jar. For a microwave of 700 watts, deduct 30 seconds' cooking time for every jar. These instructions apply to jars of any size.

Please do not home-preserve vegetables. Government health authorities warn that this could be fatal!

Always allow a space of at least 3 centimetres between jars and the oven wall.

Preserved Fruit

Equipment

The microwave method eliminates the need for elaborate equipment. A large microwave-proof bowl with a cover and a spoon, preferably wooden, are required. Jars and bottles of various shapes and sizes can be used, providing they are fitted with a rubber ring and a lid of glass or metal, plus a device that holds the lid firmly in position, such as a metal screw band, a clip or a metal spring cap.

Empty food jars are ideal for microwave bottling, as long as the lids are fitted with a built-in sealing ring. The jars must be the screw-top variety, and must not be chipped or cracked. Their rims must be smooth and free from chips, ridges and other imperfections. Damaged jars will not seal properly and the fruit will spoil.

The metal lids on most food jars are treated on the inside with a special food lacquer to protect them from corrosive food acids. It is important to check that this film is not damaged in any way and that the lids are in 'as new' condition and fit perfectly.

If you use conventional preserving jars, fit new rubber rings with each bottling. Check the clips also, as older clips tend to lose their spring and may not hold the lids firmly in place during the sealing process.

Sterilising the Equipment

1 First check that the jars you intend to use will fit in your microwave oven with their lids on.

2 Half-fill jars with cold water and cook on HIGH until water boils (approximately 2 minutes for every jar).

3 Remove jars from microwave, fill the lids of the jars with hot water. If rubber gaskets are to be used, drop each gasket into its jar of hot water for a few minutes. Pour water away before fruit is packed into jars.

4 If rubber gaskets are not to be used, pour away water.

Empty food jars are ideal for microwave bottling

Preparing & Packing the Fruit

1 Never use fruit straight from the refrigerator. Always use food at room temperature.

2 Choose unblemished fruit. Wash well in cold water.

3 Peel, core, slice or dice fruit according to recipe. Check recipe for any pre-cooking, soaking or other preparation necessary.

4 Pack fruit into clean, warm sterilised jars. Unless recipe states otherwise, leave 12 millimetres (½ inch) from lip of jar. Gently tap the bottom of each jar on the palm of your hand to ensure firm packing.

5 Fill jars to overflowing with warm syrup or other bottling liquid. Check recipes for type of liquid needed.

6 To release air from jars, ease a round-bladed knife or a special packing stick (available from stores that sell bottling equipment) down between the fruit and the inside of the jar. If necessary, top up with extra warm syrup or liquid.

7 If using clip-top jars, fit rubber gaskets in position and clip down lids. If using screw-top jars, screw lids on lightly. (Tighten lids as soon as jars are removed from oven.)

Jar Capacity

JAR SIZE	FRUIT WEIGHT	LIQUID NEEDED
250 ml (8 oz)	100 g (3 oz)	½–1 cup
400 ml (13 oz)	150 g (5 oz)	¾–1 cup
600 ml (19 oz)	300 g (10 oz)	1–1½ cups
850 ml (27 oz)	500 g (16 oz)	1½–2 cups
900 ml (29 oz)	500 g (16 oz)	2–2¼ cups

Syrup

Syrup is an important ingredient in fruit preserving. It enhances the flavour, colour and texture of the fruit.

The strength of the syrup used can be adjusted according to taste, but some fruits require heavier syrups than others for best results. The recipes in this book specify light, medium or heavy syrup.

TYPE OF SYRUP	SUGAR REQUIRED
Light syrup	one part sugar to three parts water eg 250 g (1 cup) sugar to 750 ml (3 cups) water
Medium syrup	one part sugar to two parts water eg 250 g (1 cup) sugar to 500 ml (2 cups) water
Heavy syrup	one part sugar to one part water eg 250 g (1 cup) sugar to 250 ml (1 cup) water

Making the Syrup

Place the sugar and water in a microwave-proof bowl or jug and cook in a microwave oven on HIGH. Boil for approximately 2 minutes, or until the sugar has completely dissolved. Stir once during this time.

Adding the Syrup to the Fruit

The syrup should be warm, but not boiling, when added to the jars packed with fruit. If it has cooled, cook for an additional 1–2 minutes.

Brine

Brine is sometimes used with preserved tomatoes to enhance their flavour and appearance.

To make brine, dissolve ¼ cup of cooking salt in 2½ litres (10 cups) of water.

Citric Acid

Some fruits (for example, bananas, cantaloupe, pawpaw, mangoes and figs) are low in natural fruit acids and will not preserve successfully unless citric acid is added.

The usual ratio is 3 teaspoons of citric acid to every litre (4 cups) of liquid. Check individual recipes for amounts required.

Alternative Sweeteners

SUGGESTED AMOUNTS

Honey or golden syrup	*To each cup of water add 3–4 tablespoons honey or golden syrup.*
Glucose	*To each cup of water add 125 g (4 oz) glucose*
Artificial Sweeteners	*1 Sweetener tablet for 1 cup of water*

Note: Artificial sweeteners can cause a bitter flavour after keeping. If this occurs preserve in water and sweeten as serving.

Artificial sweeteners, honey, golden syrup, glucose and natural fruit nectars or juices can be used in place of sugar. The amount of sweetener can be varied according to personal taste. But remember that excessive amounts of honey, golden syrup or brown sugar can override the fruit flavours.

Cooking the Fruit

Each recipe contains a table showing oven settings and cooking times required to bring the inside of the fruit to 83°C (180°F), thus ensuring a good seal. The times given are those needed for firm, ripe fruit at room temperature. Less cooking time is needed for soft fruits such as grapes and berries, so check cooking times of individual recipes.

Arrange jars in a circle on the carousel, leaving at least 3 centimetres (1¼ inches) between each jar.

Don't use any more than 4 jars at any one time as the cooking times will alter.

Cooling the Fruit & Checking the Seal

1 After cooking, remove jars from microwave oven and stand on a rack, board or several sheets of newspaper to cool.

2 If screw-top jars have been used, screw lids down tightly. If clip-top bottles have been used, gently press down lids without removing the clip. Use a cloth to avoid burning your hands on the hot lids.

3 Allow jars to cool for at least 1 hour or overnight before removing the spring clips.

4 Stand cold jars upside down for at least 1 hour and check for any leakage or air bubbles. The presence of either of these shows that jars have not sealed.

5 If jars have not sealed, immediately replace rubber gaskets and re-process in microwave oven for 3 minutes. Then repeat steps 1–4. If fruit is not re-processed, it must be refrigerated and eaten within 2–3 days.

6 If there is no leakage and lids remain firm, a good vacuum has been achieved and the fruit will keep well.

Storage

1 Label and date jars.

2 Store in a cool, dark place.

3 All the preserved food in this book can be kept for long periods, but for optimum colour and flavour use within 12 months.

4 Once opened, jars of preserved fruit must be stored in the refrigerator and eaten within 2–3 days.

Helpful Hints

Microwave Energy

Each and every microwave oven is just a little different, and power supplies can vary, especially at peak times or when several appliances are being run from the same circuit. The cooking times will prove to be more accurate if you clean and dry the microwave carousel before you start. Any moisture will use up microwave energy, and could affect cooking time.

Temperature

To eliminate all microbes and bacteria, fruit must reach a temperature of at least 83°C (180°F) while cooking. The times given in this book have all been tested, but you should double check them. Make sure that bubbles and activity are present during cooking time. Before removing jars from the microwave, wait until a small amount of liquid is expelled on to the carousel. This indicates that the correct temperature has been reached. If you use screw-top jars, tighten the lids as soon as you remove them from the microwave.

A List of *Do*s

- Make sure that the jars you use fit in your microwave oven.
- Choose good-quality fruit, wash well in cold water, and cut away blemishes.
- Clean jars thoroughly in hot water and remove any particles with a bottlebrush.
- Tap filled jars gently on the palm of your hand to ensure that the fruit is packed tightly.

- Completely cover the fruit with syrup or liquid, and fill each jar to overflowing. This reduces air once the lids are put on.
- To release all air from packed jars before putting on lids, gently ease a round-bladed knife or a special packing stick down between the fruit and the inside of the jar.
- Check that clips are secured firmly.
- Check that oven is set to MEDIUM HIGH for the final cooking process.
- Cool hot jars by standing them on a cake rack, a chopping board, or several sheets of newspaper to prevent cracking.
- Check that jars have sealed by turning them upside down and leaving them for at least 1 hour. If the jars do not leak, then they have sealed. If they leak, re-place rubber gaskets and cook again as shown in the recipe.   Alternatively, refrigerate and eat the fruit within 2–3 days.
- Store jars in a cool, dark place, to ensure good colour and nutritional value for a longer period.

A List of *Don't*s

- Don't worry if jars are not completely dry before packing in the fruit. Moisture helps the fruit slide into the jar.
- Don't leave rubber gaskets twisted; moisten with a little water and flick into position.
- Don't remove clips while jars are still hot; allow them to cool overnight or for several hours.
- Don't worry if a little liquid drips over the edges of jars. This is normal and safe with the microwave method and shows that excess air has been expelled and a high temperature reached.
- Don't use a bottle opener to remove lids. Always turn jars upside down, and break the seal by placing a pointed knife between the lid and rubber gasket and pressing down firmly.
- Don't re-seal half-used jars; once a jar has been opened the contents must be used within a few days.
- Don't use plastic jars or lids.

Faults & Possible Explanations & Remedies

The following advice will help you to avoid the most common mishaps and failures in microwave preserving.

FAULTS	POSSIBLE EXPLANATIONS & REMEDIES
The fruit has risen.	1 Over-ripe fruit was used. 2 The fruit was packed too loosely in the jar. 3 The jar was processed for too long. Check the table at the end of the recipe.
The fruit has a poor colour.	1 Over-ripe fruit was used. 2 The jar was processed for too long. Check the recipe for the correct cooking time. 3 Your storage area is either too light or too warm.
The jar did not seal.	1 The rubber gasket twisted. 2 The rubber gasket perished. 3 Fruit was lodged between the gasket and rim of the jar.
The jar lost its seal after storage.	1 Bruised, damaged or over-ripe fruit was used. 2 Bacteria formed. This sometimes occurs with fruit low in acids. Check the recipe for the correct quantity of acid. 3 The jar was not filled to overflowing with syrup or liquid, so air was not completely expelled. 4 The jar was not processed long enough, so a perfect seal was not obtained. Check the recipe for the correct cooking time.

Apples

INGREDIENTS
Cooking apples
Salt
Water
Medium syrup (see step 4, below)

METHOD

1

Peel and core apples, then dice, slice into circles, or quarter. Immerse in salted water (1 tablespoon of salt to 500 ml of water) to prevent discolouring.

2

When ready to use, drain and rinse fruit in fresh, cold water to remove any traces of salt.

3

Place in a microwave-proof bowl, cover with cold water and cook on HIGH. Boil for 1 minute.

4

Remove from oven and cool. Pour off water, set aside and use as syrup.

5

Pack fruit into clean, warm sterilised jars.

6

Fill jars to overflowing with medium syrup.

7

Fit lids on jars according to directions on page 6.

8

Cook according to table below.

JAR SIZE	OVEN SETTING	COOKING TIME
250–350 ml	medium high	5 mins
400–650 ml	medium high	8 mins
800–900 ml	medium high	12 mins

Note: The cooking times are for 1 jar; add 2 minutes for every additional jar.

9

Cool and store according to directions on page 10.

Apple Puree for Pies

INGREDIENTS
Cooking apples, 6–8
Water, 125 ml (½ cup)
Sugar, 250 g (1 cup)

METHOD

1
Wash apples and chop roughly. There is no need to peel or core them.

2
Place chopped fruit and water in a microwave-proof bowl and cover. Cook on HIGH until soft and pulpy (approximately 10 minutes).

3
Remove from oven and allow to stand, covered, for 5 minutes.

4
Press mixture through a sieve or Mouli, or puree in a food processor. Stir in sugar.

5
Fill clean, warm sterilised jars to brim with apple pulp.

6
Fit lids on jars according to directions on page 6.

7
Cook according to table below.

JAR SIZE	OVEN SETTING	COOKING TIME
250–350 ml	*medium high*	*3 mins*
400–650 ml	*medium high*	*3 mins*
800–900 ml	*medium high*	*4 mins*

Note: The cooking times are for 1 jar; add 2 minutes for every additional jar.

8
Cool and store according to directions on page 10.

Apricots

INGREDIENTS
Apricots
Medium syrup

METHOD

1
Choose firm, ripe unblemished apricots and wash. They can be halved or, if small, left whole. To halve, cut around the natural line with a stainless steel knife and twist apart. Remove and discard stones.

2
Pack fruit into clean, warm sterilised jars.

3
Fill jars to overflowing with medium syrup.

4
Fit lids on jars according to directions on page 6.

5
Cook according to table below.

JAR SIZE	OVEN SETTING	COOKING TIME
250–350 ml	medium high	5 mins
400–600 ml	medium high	8 mins
700–900 ml	medium high	12 mins

Note: The cooking times are for 1 jar; add 2 minutes for every additional jar.

6
Cool and store according to directions on page 10.

Apricot Puree for Pies

INGREDIENTS
Apricots, 1 kg (2 lbs)
Water, 250 ml (1 cup)
Sugar, 250 g (1 cup)

METHOD

1

Wash apricots and halve by cutting around the natural line with a stainless steel knife. Twist halves apart. Remove and discard stones.

2

Place fruit and water in a microwave-proof bowl and cover. Cook on HIGH until soft and pulpy (approximately 7 minutes).

3

Remove from oven and allow to stand, covered, for 5 minutes.

4

Press mixture through a sieve or a mouli, or puree in a food processor. Stir in sugar.

5

Fill clean, warm sterilised jars to brim with apricot pulp.

6

Fit lids on jars according to directions on page 6.

7

Cook according to table below.

SIZE	OVEN SETTING	COOKING TIME
250–350 ml	medium high	3 mins
400–650 ml	medium high	3 mins
700–900 ml	medium high	4 mins

Note: The cooking times are for 1 jar; add 2 minutes for every additional jar.

8

Cool and store according to directions on page 10.

Spicy Apricots & Almonds

INGREDIENTS
Apricots
Almonds, at least 2 for each apricot
Mixed spice, ½ teaspoon for every 250 ml (1 cup) of syrup
Medium syrup

METHOD

1

Blanch almonds by placing them in a microwave-proof bowl, covering them with water and heating on HIGH for 2–3 minutes. Cool, then squeeze almonds between fingers to remove brown skins.

2

Pack prepared apricots into clean, warm sterilised jars, placing almonds between each piece of fruit.

3

Add mixed spice to syrup.

4

Fill jars to overflowing with syrup mixture.

5

Fit lids on jars according to directions on page 6.

6

Cook according to table below.

JAR SIZE	OVEN SETTING	COOKING TIME
250–350 ml	medium high	5 mins
400–650 ml	medium high	8 mins
700–900 ml	medium high	12 mins

Note: The cooking times are for 1 jar; add 2 minutes for every additional jar.

7

Cool and store according to directions on page 10.

Bananas

INGREDIENTS
Bananas
Citric acid, 1 teaspoon for every 750 ml (3 cups) of syrup
Medium syrup

METHOD

1
Choose firm, ripe bananas with no bruises or blemishes. Peel under cold water to prevent discolouring. Pat dry when ready to use.

2
Cut into thick slices or lengths to fit selected jars.

3
Pack fruit into clean, warm sterilised jars.

4
Dissolve citric acid in medium syrup.

5
Fill jars to overflowing with syrup mixture.

6
Fit lids on jars according to directions on page 6.

7
Cook according to table below.

JAR SIZE	OVEN SETTING	COOKING TIME
250–350 ml	medium high	4 mins
400–650 ml	medium high	4 mins
700–900 ml	medium high	5 mins

Note: The cooking times are for 1 jar; add 2 minutes for every additional jar.

8
Cool and store according to directions on page 10.

Berries

INGREDIENTS
Berries (strawberries, raspberries, loganberries, blackberries,
blueberries, etc.)
Sugar, an equal weight to berries

METHOD

1
Choose whole, ripe berries with no blemishes. Remove any
husks, clean in cold water and drain.

2
Place fruit and sugar in a microwave-proof bowl and cover.
Cook on HIGH for 1 minute.

3
Remove from oven, cover and cool.

4
Pack fruit into clean, warm sterilised jars.

5
Fit lids on jars according to directions on page 6.

6
Cook according to table below.

JAR SIZE	OVEN SETTING	COOKING TIME
250–350 ml	medium high	3 mins
400–650 ml	medium high	3 mins
700–900 ml	medium high	5 mins

*Note: The cooking times are for 1 jar; add 2 minutes for every
additional jar.*

Cool and store according to directions on page 10.

Cantaloupe

INGREDIENTS
Cantaloupe
Citric acid, 3 teaspoons for every litre (4 cups) of syrup
Medium syrup

METHOD

1
Choose a firm, ripe cantaloupe. Peel and seed. Round out small balls with a melon baller, slice or dice.

2
Pack fruit into clean, warm sterilised jars.

3
Dissolve citric acid in medium syrup.

4
Fill jars to overflowing with syrup mixture.

5
Fit lids on jars according to directions on page 6.

6
Cook according to table below.

JAR SIZE	OVEN SETTING	COOKING TIME
250–350 ml	medium high	4 mins
400–650 ml	medium high	5 mins
700–900 ml	medium high	6 mins

Note: The cooking times are for 1 jar; add 2 minutes for every additional jar.

7
Cool and store according to directions on page 10.

Cherries

INGREDIENTS
Cherries
Medium syrup

METHOD

1
Discard any damaged or blemished cherries and wash the rest clean. If desired, remove stones with a cherry stoner.

2
Pack fruit into clean, warm sterilised jars.

3
Fill jars to overflowing with medium syrup.

4
Fit lids on jars according to directions on page 6.

5
Cook according to table below.

JAR SIZE	OVEN SETTING	COOKING TIME
250–350 ml	*medium high*	*5 mins*
400–650 ml	*medium high*	*8 mins*
700–900 ml	*medium high*	*12 mins*

Note: The cooking times are for 1 jar; add 2 minutes for every additional jar.

6
Cool and store according to directions on page 10.

Cumquats

INGREDIENTS
Cumquats
Heavy syrup

METHOD

1

Wash cumquats in cold water, then prick each fruit all over
with a large needle.

2

Pack fruit into clean, warm sterilised jars.

3

Fill jars to overflowing with heavy syrup.

4

Fit lids on jars according to directions on page 6.

5

Cook according to table below.

JAR SIZE	OVEN SETTING	COOKING TIME
250–350 ml	medium high	4 mins
400–650 ml	medium high	6 mins
700–900 ml	medium high	8 mins

*Note: The cooking times are for 1 jar; add 2 minutes for every
additional jar.*

6

Cool and store according to directions on page 10.

Figs

INGREDIENTS
Figs
Citric acid, 1 teaspoon for every litre (4 cups) of syrup
Heavy syrup

METHOD

1

Wash figs and wipe dry. Pierce the skin in several places with the point of a small, sharp knife. This allows the syrup to penetrate fruit during storage.

2

Pack fruit into clean, warm sterilised jars.

3

Dissolve citric acid in heavy syrup.

4

Fill jars to overflowing with syrup mixture.

5

Fit lids on jars according to directions on page 6.

6

Cook according to table below.

JAR SIZE	OVEN SETTING	COOKING TIME
250–350 ml	medium high	3 mins
400–650 ml	medium high	4 mins
800–900 ml	medium high	6 mins

Note: The cooking times are for 1 jar; add 2 minutes for every additional jar.

7

Cool and store according to directions on page 10.

Fruit Salad

INGREDIENTS
Variety of fruits high in citric acid (apples, apricots, cherries,
grapes, pineapples, peaches and oranges)
Medium syrup

METHOD

1

Choose ripe fruits high in citric acid. Fresh fruits low in
citric acid (such as bananas, cantaloupes, pawpaws, figs
and mangoes) can be added when preserved fruit salad is
served.

2

Peel fruit, if necessary, and cut or dice. Mix together.

3

Pack fruit into clean, warm sterilised jars.

4

Fill jars to overflowing with medium syrup.

5

Fit lids on jars according to directions on page 6.

6

Cook according to table below.

JAR SIZE	OVEN SETTING	COOKING TIME
250–350 ml	medium high	4 mins
400–650 ml	medium high	5 mins
700–900 ml	medium high	6 mins

*Note: The cooking times are for 1 jar; add 2 minutes for every
additional jar.*

7

Cool and store according to directions on page 10.

Grapefruit in Spiced Brandy

INGREDIENTS
Grapefruit
Mixed spice, ¼ teaspoon for every 250 ml (1 cup) of syrup
Brandy, 1 tablespoon for every 250 ml (1 cup) of syrup
Medium syrup

METHOD

1
Peel grapefruits and remove pith. Divide into segments, strip skin away from each segment and remove any seeds.

2
Pack fruit into clean, warm sterilised jars.

3
Add mixed spice and brandy to medium syrup.

4
Fill jars to overflowing with syrup mixture.

5
Fit lids on jars according to directions on page 6.

6
Cook according to table below.

JAR SIZE	OVEN SETTING	COOKING TIME
250–350 ml	medium high	3 mins
400–650 ml	medium high	5 mins
700–900 ml	medium high	8 mins

Note: The cooking times are for 1 jar; add 2 minutes for every additional jar.

7
Cool and store according to directions on page 10.

Grapes

INGREDIENTS
Grapes
Medium syrup

METHOD

1

Choose firm, unblemished grapes. Seedless sultana grapes are the most convenient to use. Wash fruit and remove any stalks. If using grapes with seeds, push rounded end of a sterilised bobby pin into hole left by stalk and pull out seeds.

2

Pack fruit into clean, warm sterilised jars.

3

Fill jars to overflowing with medium syrup.

4

Fit lids on jars according to directions on page 6.

5

Cook according to table below.

JAR SIZE	OVEN SETTING	COOKING TIME
250–350 ml	medium high	3 mins
400–650 ml	medium high	5 mins
700–900 ml	medium high	8 mins

Note: The cooking times are for 1 jar; add 2 minutes for every additional jar.

6

Cool and store according to directions on page 10.

Honey Brandy Grapes

INGREDIENTS
Grapes
Honey, 1 tablespoon for every 250 ml (1 cup) of syrup
Brandy, 1 tablespoon for every 250 ml (1 cup) of syrup
Medium syrup

METHOD

1

Choose firm, unblemished grapes. Seedless sultana grapes are the most convenient to use. Wash fruit and remove any stalks. If using grapes with seeds, push rounded end of a sterilised bobby pin into hole left by stalk and pull out seeds.

2

Pack fruit into clean, warm sterilised jars.

3

Stir honey and brandy into warm medium syrup.

4

Fill jars to overflowing with syrup mixture.

5

Fit lids on jars according to directions on page 6.

6

Cook according to table below.

JAR SIZE	OVEN SETTING	COOKING TIME
250–350 ml	medium high	3 mins
400–650 ml	medium high	5 mins
700–900 ml	medium high	8 mins

Note: The cooking times are for 1 jar; add 2 minutes for every additional jar.

7

Cool and store according to directions on page 10.

Mandarins

INGREDIENTS
Mandarins
Medium syrup

METHOD

1
Choose fresh, ripe unblemished fruit. Peel, divide into segments and remove stringy pith. Strip skin away from each segment and remove any seeds.

2
Pack fruit into clean, warm sterilised jars.

3
Fill jars to overflowing with medium syrup.

4
Fit lids on jars according to directions on page 6.

5
Cook according to table below.

JAR SIZE	OVEN SETTING	COOKING TIME
250–350 ml	medium high	3 mins
400–650 ml	medium high	5 mins
700–900 ml	medium high	8 mins

Note: The cooking times are for 1 jar; add 2 minutes for every additional jar.

6
Cool and store according to directions on page 10.

Orange Segments

INGREDIENTS
Oranges
Medium syrup

METHOD

1
Peel oranges and remove pith. Divide into segments, strip skin away from each segment and remove any seeds.

2
Pack fruit into clean, warm sterilised jars.

3
Fill jars to overflowing with medium syrup.

4
Fit lids on jars according to directions on page 6.

5
Cook according to table below.

JAR SIZE	OVEN SETTING	COOKING TIME
250–350 ml	medium high	3 mins
400–650 ml	medium high	5 mins
700–900 ml	medium high	8 mins

Note: The cooking times are for 1 jar; add 2 minutes for every additional jar.

6
Cool and store according to directions on page 10.

Pawpaw (Papaya) with Curacao

INGREDIENTS
Pawpaw (papaya), 1 small ripe fruit
Sugar, 4 tablespoons
Water, 1 teaspoon
Citric acid, ½ teaspoon
White curacao, 180 ml (¾ cup)

METHOD

1
Peel pawpaws, cut in half and scoop out seeds. Cut into slices or cubes.

2
Pack fruit into clean, warm sterilised jars.

3
Place sugar and water in a microwave-proof bowl and cook on HIGH for 1 minute, or until sugar dissolves. Cool, add citric acid and curacao and stir.

4
Fill jars to overflowing with liquid.

5
Fit lids on jars according to directions on page 6.

6
Cook according to table below.

JAR SIZE	OVEN SETTING	COOKING TIME
250–350 ml	medium high	4 mins
400–650 ml	medium high	5 mins
700–900 ml	medium high	6 mins

Note: The cooking times are for 1 jar; add 2 minutes for every additional jar.

7
Cool and store according to directions on page 10.

Pawpaw (Papaya)

INGREDIENTS
Pawpaw (papaya)
Citric acid, 2 teaspoons for every litre (4 cups) of medium syrup
Medium syrup

METHOD

1
Peel pawpaw, cut in half and scoop out seeds. Cut into slices or cubes.

2
Pack fruit into clean, warm sterilised jars.

3
Dissolve citric acid in medium syrup.

4
Fill jars to overflowing with syrup mixture.

5
Fit lids on jars according to directions on page 6.

6
Cook according to table below.

JAR SIZE	OVEN SETTING	COOKING TIME
250–350 ml	medium high	3 mins
400–650 ml	medium high	4 mins
700–900 ml	medium high	5 mins

Note: The cooking times are for 1 jar; add 2 minutes for every additional jar.

7
Cool and store according to directions on page 10.

Peaches (Clingstone & Freestone)

INGREDIENTS
Peaches
Medium syrup

METHOD

1
Peel peaches with a stainless steel knife or peeling utensil. Alternatively, immerse peaches in boiling water for 2 minutes, then dip in cold water and pull off skins.

2
Leave fruit whole, or halve or slice. To remove stones from clingstone peaches, insert a round-bladed knife or a peach pitting spoon at stalk end, and cut flesh away from stone. To remove stones from freestone peaches, cut around natural line of fruit and twist apart.

3
Pack fruit into clean, warm sterilised jars.

4
Fill jars to overflowing with medium syrup.

5
Fit lids on jars according to directions on page 6.

6
Cook according to table below.

JAR SIZE	OVEN SETTING	COOKING TIME
250–350 ml	medium high	5 mins
400–650 ml	medium high	8 mins
700–900 ml	medium high	12 mins

Note: The cooking times are for 1 jar; add 2 minutes for every additional jar.

7
Cool and store according to directions on page 10.

Peaches in Brandy
(Clingstone & Freestone)

INGREDIENTS
Peaches
Brandy, 1 tablespoon for every 250 ml (1 cup) of syrup
Medium syrup

METHOD

1
Peel peaches with a stainless steel knife or peeling utensil.
Alternatively, immerse peaches in boiling water for 2
minutes, then dip in cold water and pull off skins.

2
Leave whole, or halve or slice. To remove stones from
clingstone peaches, insert a round-bladed knife or a peach
pitting spoon at stalk end, and cut flesh away from stone.
To remove stones from freestone peaches, cut around
natural line of fruit and twist apart.

3
Pack fruit into clean, warm sterilised jars.

4
Add brandy to medium syrup.

5
Fill jars to overflowing with syrup mixture.

6
Fit lids on jars according to directions on page 6.

7
Cook according to table below.

JAR SIZE	*OVEN SETTING*	*COOKING TIME*
250–350 ml	*medium high*	*5 mins*
400–650 ml	*medium high*	*8 mins*
700–900 ml	*medium high*	*12 mins*

*Note: The cooking times are for 1 jar; add 2 minutes for every
additional jar.*

8
Cool and store according to directions on page 10.

Pears

INGREDIENTS
Pears
Salt
Water
Lemon strips
Medium syrup

METHOD

1

Peel, core and cut pears in half. If not using immediately, place in salted water (1 tablespoon of salt to 2 cups of water) to prevent discolouring. When ready to use, drain pear pieces and rinse in fresh, cold water to remove salt.

2

Pack fruit into clean, warm sterilised jars.

3

Fill jars to overflowing with medium syrup.

4

Add 2–3 lemon strips to every jar to enhance colour while stored.

5

Fit lids on jars according to directions on page 6.

6

Cook according to table below.

JAR SIZE	OVEN SETTING	COOKING TIME
250–350 ml	medium high	5 mins
400–650 ml	medium high	8 mins
700–900 ml	medium high	12 mins

Note: The cooking times are for 1 jar; add 2 minutes for every additional jar.

7

Cool and store according to directions on page 10.

Pears with Green Ginger

INGREDIENTS
Pears
Salt
Water
Green ginger, 60 g (2 oz) for every 3–4 pears
Medium syrup

METHOD

1
Peel, core and cut pears in half. If not using immediately, place in salted water (1 tablespoon of salt to 2 cups of water) to prevent discolouring. When ready to use, drain pear pieces and rinse in fresh, cold water to remove salt.

2
Peel ginger, cut into thin slices and cook in 1 cup of water on HIGH until tender (approximately 6–8 minutes).

3
Pack fruit and ginger into clean, warm sterilised jars.

4
Fill jars to overflowing with medium syrup.

5
Fit lids on jars according to directions on page 6.

6
Cook according to table below.

JAR SIZE	OVEN SETTING	COOKING TIME
250–350 ml	medium high	5 mins
400–650 ml	medium high	8 mins
700–900 ml	medium high	12 mins

Note: The cooking times are for 1 jar; add 2 minutes for every additional jar.

7
Cool and store according to directions on page 10.

Pineapple

INGREDIENTS
Pineapple
Medium syrup

METHOD

1
Peel, eye and core pineapple. Cut into cubes, wedges or circles.

2
Pack fruit into clean, warm sterilised jars.

3
Fill jars to overflowing with medium syrup.

4
Fit lids on jars according to directions on page 6.

5
Cook according to table below.

JAR SIZE	OVEN SETTING	COOKING TIME
250–350 ml	medium high	5 mins
400–650 ml	medium high	8 mins
700–900 ml	medium high	12 mins

Note: The cooking times are for 1 jar; add 2 minutes for every additional jar.

6
Cool and store according to directions on page 10.

Pineapple & Passionfruit

INGREDIENTS
Pineapple
Passionfruit, 4–6
Medium syrup

METHOD

1
Peel, eye and core pineapple. Cut into cubes, wedges or circles. Remove pulp from passionfruit and stir into pineapple pieces.

2
Pack fruit into clean, warm sterilised jars.

3
Fill jars to overflowing with medium syrup.

4
Fit lids on jars according to directions on page 6.

5
Cook according to table below.

JAR SIZE	OVEN SETTING	COOKING TIME
250–350 ml	medium high	5 mins
400–650 ml	medium high	8 mins
700–900 ml	medium high	12 mins

Note: The cooking times are for 1 jar; add 2 minutes for every additional jar.

6
Cool and store according to directions on page 10.

Plums

INGREDIENTS
Plums
Medium syrup

METHOD

1

When using whole plums wash and prick all over with a needle to prevent skins from splitting when cooked. Cut around the natural line of fruit and twist halves apart. Remove and discard stones.

2

Pack fruit into clean, warm sterilised jars.

3

Fill jars to overflowing with medium syrup.

4

Fit lids on jars according to directions on page 6.

5

Cook according to table below.

JAR SIZE	*OVEN SETTING*	*COOKING TIME*
250–350 ml	*medium high*	*5 mins*
400–650 ml	*medium high*	*8 mins*
700–900 ml	*medium high*	*12 mins*

Note: The cooking times are for 1 jar; add 2 minutes for every additional jar.

6

Cool and store according to directions on page 10.

Quinces

INGREDIENTS
Quinces
Salt
Water
Heavy syrup

METHOD

1
Peel, core and quarter quinces, then slice or dice. If not using immediately, place in salted water (1 tablespoon of salt to 2 cups of water) to prevent discolouring. When ready to use, drain and rinse in fresh, cold water to remove salt.

2
Place quinces and heavy syrup in a microwave-proof bowl and cook on MEDIUM HIGH at boiling point for 4–5 minutes. Cool.

3
Pack fruit into clean, warm sterilised jars.

4
Fill jars to overflowing with heavy syrup.

5
Fit lids on jars according to directions on page 6.

6
Cook according to table below.

JAR SIZE	OVEN SETTING	COOKING TIME
250–350 ml	medium high	3 mins
400–650 ml	medium high	4 mins
700–900 ml	medium high	5 mins

Note: The cooking times are for 1 jar; add 2 minutes for every additional jar.

7
Cool and store according to directions on page 10.

Rhubarb

INGREDIENTS
Rhubarb
Heavy syrup

METHOD

1
Choose young, tender rhubarb stalks.

2
Trim away base and leaves, and cut stalks into 3 cm
(1¼ inch) lengths.

3
Pack stalks into clean, warm sterilised jars.

4
Fill jars to overflowing with heavy syrup.

5
Fit lids on jars according to directions on page 6.

6
Cook according to table below.

JAR SIZE	OVEN SETTING	COOKING TIME
250–350 ml	medium high	5 mins
400–650 ml	medium high	8 mins
700–900 ml	medium high	12 mins

*Note: The cooking times are for 1 jar; add 2 minutes for every
additional jar.*

7
Cool and store according to directions on page 10.

Tomatoes

INGREDIENTS
Tomatoes
Brine, 30 g (1 oz) salt for every 1.25 litres (5 cups) of water

METHOD

1

Immerse tomatoes in boiling water for 2–3 minutes, then
place in cold water and peel off skins.

2

Pack fruit into clean, warm sterilised jars.

3

Fill jars to overflowing with brine.

4

Fit lids on jars according to directions on page 6.

5

Cook according to table below.

JAR SIZE	OVEN SETTING	COOKING TIME
250–350 ml	*medium high*	*5 mins*
400–650 ml	*medium high*	*8 mins*
700–900 ml	*medium high*	*12 mins*

*Note: The cooking times are for 1 jar; add 2 minutes for every
additional jar.*

6

Repeat step 5 on following day.

7

Cool and store according to directions on page 10.

Tomato Pulp

INGREDIENTS
Tomatoes
Brine, 30 g (2 oz) *salt for every 1.25 litres (5 cups) of water*

METHOD

1
Immerse tomatoes in boiling water for 2–3 minutes, then place in cold water and peel off skins.

2
Cut up tomatoes roughly.

3
Pack fruit into clean, warm sterilised jars.

4
Fill jars to overflowing with brine.

5
Fit lids on jars according to directions on page 6.

6
Cook according to table below.

JAR SIZE	OVEN SETTING	COOKING TIME
250–350 ml	*medium high*	*5 mins*
400–650 ml	*medium high*	*8 mins*
700–900 ml	*medium high*	*12 mins*

Note: The cooking times are for 1 jar; add 2 minutes for every additional jar.

7
Repeat step 6 on following day.

8
Cool and store according to directions on page 10.

Two Fruits

INGREDIENTS
Suggested combinations: peach and pear, peach and apricot,
pineapple and apricot, berry and diced apple, quince and apple.*
Medium syrup

METHOD

1
Choose ripe, unblemished fruit and prepare as required.

2
Pack fruit into clean, warm sterilised jars.

3
Fill jars to overflowing with medium syrup.

4
Fit lids on jars according to directions on page 6.

5
Cook according to table below.

JAR SIZE	OVEN SETTING	COOKING TIME
250–350 ml	medium high	5 mins
400–650 ml	medium high	8 mins
700–900 ml	medium high	12 mins

Note: The cooking times are for 1 jar; add 2 minutes for every additional jar.

6
Cool and store according to directions on page 10.

Note: Do not use fruit low in citric acid, such as bananas, cantaloupe, figs, pawpaw and mango.

2

Jams, Marmalades, Jellies & Conserves

Jams, marmalades, jellies and conserves can be made quickly, easily and economically in the microwave oven. The process enhances the taste and colour of the fruit.

You don't need a large amount of fruit for the microwave method. In fact, about 2 kilograms (5 pounds) is an ideal quantity for best results. Any more than this amount tends to negate the time-saving and other benefits of the microwave method.

Similarly, very little additional water is needed in the microwave method, so the natural flavour and colour of the fruits are preserved.

It is impossible to give exact cooking times — the type of fruit used, its condition and degree of ripeness will determine the cooking times. The times given are as accurate as possible. If you follow the method and test the mixture when you think it is ready, you should achieve good results.

Equipment

All types of jams, marmalades, jellies and conserves require the same simple equipment.

1 A large, microwave-proof bowl with a cover.

2 A large spoon, preferably wooden.

3 Clean jars, free of chips, ridges or other imperfections, and sufficient covers or screw-top lids to fit.

Sterilising the Equipment

1 Check that the jars you intend to use will fit in microwave oven with their lids on.

2 Half-fill jars with water, place in oven and cook on

HIGH until water boils (approximately 2 minutes for each jar).

3 Remove jars from oven and pour away water. Any excess water will evaporate as the jars cool.

Warming the Jars

To achieve the best results, warm the jars before you fill them with the cooked fruit mixture. This should be done after the mixture is ready, just before filling the jars.

1 Cover bases of jars with water.

2 Place in microwave oven and cook on HIGH until water boils.

3 Pour off any excess water just before filling jars.

The following tables will help you determine the proportion of sugar to fruit pulp to use when making jams with fresh fruit, marmalades, jellies and conserves. Jams made with preserved fruit require less sugar; check table under relevant section for the required amount of sugar.

Sugar ratios

SUGAR REQUIRED FOR HIGH & MEDIUM PECTIN FRUITS

SUGAR	FRUIT PULP
1 cup	2 cups
2 cups	2 cups
3 cups	3 cups
4 cups	4 cups
5 cups	5 cups
6 cups	6 cups
7 cups	7 cups

SUGAR REQUIRED FOR LOW PECTIN FRUITS

SUGAR	FRUIT PULP
1½ cups	2 cups
2¼ cups	3 cups
3 cups	4 cups

SUGAR	FRUIT PULP
3¾ cups	5 cups
4½ cups	6 cups
5¼ cups	7 cups
6 cups	8 cups

Note: Always use the same sized cup to measure the fruit pulp and sugar.

Setting Point

It is essential to test mixtures to make sure that setting point has been reached, otherwise the product will be runny and unusable. The following steps are common to all jams, marmalades, jellies and conserves.

1 Before preparing fruit, place a saucer in the refrigerator.

2 Remove bowl of cooked fruit from microwave. (If you continue cooking fruit while testing a sample, it may be cooked beyond setting point, spoiling the flavour, texture and colour of the final product.)

3 Put a teaspoon of hot mixture on cold saucer and cool. When cool, surface should crinkle when saucer is tilted slightly.

4 If test is not positive, return bowl to microwave and cook on HIGH for a few more minutes. Repeat test.

Vacuum Sealing

Vacuum sealing expels the air from filled jars and seals them. While it is not essential to vacuum seal jams, the process will ensure the longest possible keeping time.

1 Choose screw-top jars with built-in sealing rings or inserts.

2 After you fill the jars, cover them with screw-top lids, but do not screw them down tightly.

3 While filled jars are still hot, place them in micro-wave, about 5 centimeters (2 inches) apart, and cook on MEDIUM HIGH for 2–3 minutes. Remove jars from microwave and place on a towel, several sheets

of newspaper or a chopping board to prevent cracking. Screw lids down tightly, protecting your hands with a towel or an oven mitt, and cool.

4 When cool, the lids will be slightly concave, showing that a vacuum seal has been achieved.

Storage

Store jams, marmalades, jellies and conserves in a cool, dark place. This retards the growth of mould. If mould does form, remove and discard. Place remaining mixture in a microwave-proof bowl and cook on HIGH at boiling point for 2–3 minutes. Re-bottle in clean, warm jars and vacuum seal.

Pectin & Fruit Acids

Pectin, a naturally occurring fruit acid, is a vital element in jams, marmalades, jellies and conserves. Without pectin, they would not set. The highest quantities of pectin occur in fruits that are firm and just under-ripe (pectin in over-ripe fruit converts to sugar).

Fruits that have high levels of acid are ideal, as the acid inhibits the growth of bacteria and prevents the formation of toxins. Natural fruit acids are also necessary because they draw out pectin, improve the flavour of the fruit and help prevent crystallisation.

If the fruit is over-ripe, or naturally low in pectin or other fruit acids, lemon juice or citric acid must be added. The amounts required are specified in the recipes.

HIGH PECTIN FRUITS	MEDIUM PECTIN FRUITS	LOW PECTIN FRUITS
cooking apples	apricots	bananas
crab-apples	blackberries	ripe cherries
quinces	under-ripe cherries	figs
citrus fruits:	loganberries	grapes
cumquats	greengage plums	peaches
grapefruits	ripe plums	pears
lemons	pineapples	strawberries
oranges	rhubarb	

Testing Pectin Content

Place a teaspoon of cooked or preserved fruit in 3 tea-spoons of methylated spirits and leave for 2 minutes until mixture clots and becomes firm.

Large, firm clots indicate high pectin content. Medium-sized clots which are not so firm indicate medium pectin content. Weak, flabby clots indicate low pectin content.

Overcoming Pectin Deficiency

Sweet, over-ripe fruits and fruits low in pectin can be used in jams, marmalades, jellies and conserves if one of the following steps is taken:

1 Add 2 tablespoons of lemon juice to every kilogram (4 cups) of fruit.

2 Add 1 teaspoon of citric acid to every kilogram (4 cups) of fruit.

3 Add commercially produced pectin, following the manufacturer's directions.

Sugar

White granulated sugar is the most popular variety used to make jams, marmalades, jellies and conserves. Sugar cubes can be used, but it is difficult to measure the correct proportion of sugar to fruit. Jam can crystal-lise if too much sugar is used, and it can ferment if too little sugar is used.

Brown sugar can be used but it makes the fruit darker, so it should be used only for darker coloured fruits such as plums or blackcurrants.

Fruits with high or moderate pectin content (see page 69) require equal amounts of sugar and fruit pulp, for example, 1 cup of sugar to 1 cup of fruit.

Fruits with low pectin content require ¾ the amount of sugar to fruit pulp, for example, ¾ cup of sugar to 1 cup of fruit.

Jams Made with Fresh Fruit

Method

1
Choose firm fruit which is a little under-ripe and free of blemishes. Cut away and discard bruised areas.

2
Wash fruit, peel if necessary, cut into halves and remove any pips or stones.

3
Add lemon juice or citric acid, if required.

4
Add water.

5
Place fruit mixture in a microwave-proof bowl, cover and cook on HIGH until soft and pulpy.

6
Remove bowl from oven and measure fruit pulp. If pulp has cooled, re-heat. Stir in required amount of sugar (see table on page 48), making sure that sugar is dissolved. Add spices, if required.

7
Return uncovered mixture to microwave and cook on HIGH for approximately 15–20 minutes until setting point has been reached (see page 49).

8
Skim jam to remove any scum.

9
Fill clean, warm sterilised jars to the brim.

10
Fit lids on jars immediately. Do not allow jam to cool, as warm jam will form condensation, causing mould.

11
Label and date jars.

12
Store in a cool, dark place.

Apricot Jam

INGREDIENTS
Apricots, 1 kg (2 lbs)
Water, 500 ml (2 cups)
Sugar

METHOD

Follow directions on page 52.

Apricot & Pineapple Jam

INGREDIENTS
Apricots, 1 kg (2 lbs)
Crushed fresh pineapple, 500 ml (2 cups)
Water, 250 ml (1 cup)
Sugar

METHOD

Follow directions on page 52.

Apple & Blackberry Jam

INGREDIENTS
Cooking apples, 1 kg (2 lbs)
Blackberries, 1 kg (2 lbs)
Water, 250 ml (1 cup)
Sugar
Lemon juice, 3 tablespoons
or
Citric acid, 1½ teaspoons

METHOD

Follow directions on page 52.

Cherry Jam

INGREDIENTS
Cherries, 1 kg (2 lbs)
Water, 125 ml (½ cup)
Sugar
Lemon juice, 2 tablespoons
or
Citric acid, 1 teaspoon

METHOD

Follow directions on page 52.

Fig Jam

INGREDIENTS
Figs, 1 kg (2 lbs)
Water, 185 ml (¾ cup)
Sugar
Lemon juice, 3 tablespoons
or
Citric acid, 1½ teaspoons
Ginger, peeled and finely chopped, 1 tablespoon

METHOD

Follow directions on page 52.

Pineapple Jam

INGREDIENTS
Pineapple, 1 kg (2 lbs)
Water, 125 ml (½ cup)
Sugar
Lemon juice, 2 tablespoons
or
Citric acid, 1 teaspoon

METHOD

Follow directions on page 52.

Jam Made with Preserved Fruit

If too much preserved fruit accumulates in your cupboard, don't despair; preserved fruit is ideal for making jam. The process is quicker than using fresh fruit, and the results are cheaper and tastier than commercially produced jams.

Because preserved fruits do not have seeds or stones, and the skins have softened, the process is easier and quicker. If your jam supply is depleted you can renew it in 15–20 minutes. By using preserved fruit to make jam, you can make relatively small quantities of a variety of flavours.

Sugar

Preserved fruits in syrup already contain some sugar, so the proportion of sugar to fruit pulp is reduced.

The following tables will help you determine the proportion of sugar to fruit pulp.

SUGAR REQUIRED FOR FRUIT BOTTLED IN MEDIUM SYRUP

SUGAR	FRUIT PULP & SYRUP
½ cup	1 cup
¾ cup	1½ cups
1 cup	2 cups
1¼ cups	2½ cups
1½ cups	3 cups
1¾ cups	3½ cups
2 cups	4 cups

SUGAR REQUIRED FOR FRUIT BOTTLED IN HEAVY SYRUP

SUGAR	FRUIT PULP & SYRUP
¼ cup	1 cup
½ cup	1½ cups
¾ cup	2 cups
1 cup	2½ cups
1½ cups	3 cups
1¾ cups	3½ cups
2 cups	4 cups

Method

The following steps are standard for all jams made with preserved fruit, but check recipes for minor variations.

1

Transfer fruit and syrup from jar to a microwave-proof bowl.

2

Mash fruit into a coarse pulp, using a fork or a potato masher.

3

Cover bowl and cook on HIGH until mixture boils.

4

Remove bowl from microwave and add required amount of sugar (see table on page 48). Stir until dissolved. Add lemon juice or citric acid, if required.

5

Return uncovered mixture to microwave and cook on HIGH for approximately 15–20 minutes until setting point has been reached (see page 49).

6

Fill clean, warm sterilised jars to brim with jam.

7

Fit lids on jars immediately. Do not allow jam to cool, as warm jam will create condensation, causing mould.

8

Label and date jars.

9

Store in a cool, dark place.

Fig Jam

INGREDIENTS
Preserved figs, 700–900 ml jar
Sugar
Lemon juice, 3 tablespoons
or
Citric acid, 1½ teaspoons

METHOD

Follow directions on page 56.

Peach Jam

INGREDIENTS
Preserved peaches, 700–900 ml jar
Sugar
Lemon juice, 3 tablespoons
or
Citric acid, 1½ teaspoons

METHOD

Follow directions on page 56.

Pear & Ginger Jam

INGREDIENTS
Preserved pears, 700–900 ml jar
Fresh ginger, peeled and finely chopped, 2 tablespoons
Sugar
Lemon juice, 3 tablespoons
or
Citric acid, 1½ teaspoons

METHOD

Follow directions on page 56.

Marmalades

Method

The following steps are standard for all marmalades made with fresh fruit, but check recipes for minor variations.

1
Wash fruit and slice thinly.

2
Cover with water and let stand overnight, or for several hours.

3
Place fruit and water in a microwave-proof bowl, cover and cook on HIGH until rind is tender (approximately 6–10 minutes).

4
Strain to remove pips and rind. Retain desired amount of rind.

5
Measure strained mixture.

6
Re-heat mixture on HIGH to boiling point. Stir in required amount of sugar (see table on page 48, but check recipe for variations) until dissolved.

7
Return uncovered mixture to microwave and cook on HIGH for approximately 15–20 minutes until setting point has been reached (see page 49).

8
Fill clean, warm sterilised, jars to brim with marmalade.

9
Fit lids on jars immediately. Do not allow marmalade to cool, as warm marmalade will create condensation, causing mould to grow.

10
Label and date jars.

11
Store in a cool, dark place.

Breakfast Brandy Marmalade

INGREDIENTS
Oranges, 3 large
Lemons, 2 large
Water, 1 litre (4 cups)
Brandy, 60 ml (¼ cup)
Sugar

METHOD

Follow directions on page 58.
Note: Add brandy at step 2.

Ginger & Lemon Marmalade

INGREDIENTS
Lemons, 3 large
Preserved ginger, finely chopped, ½ cup
Water, 1 litre (4 cups)
Sugar

METHOD

Follow directions on page 58.

Lime Marmalade

INGREDIENTS
Limes, 8–10
Water, 1.25 litres (5 cups)
Sugar

METHOD

Follow directions on page 58.

Orange Marmalade

INGREDIENTS
Oranges, 3 large
Lemon juice, 60 ml (¼ cup)
Water, 750 ml (3 cups)
Sugar

METHOD

Follow directions on page 58.
Note: Add lemon at step 6.

Pineapple Marmalade

INGREDIENTS
Fresh pineapple, finely chopped, 3 cups
Oranges, 2
Lemon, 1
Water, 1 litre (4 cups)
Sugar

METHOD

Follow directions on page 58.
Notes: Allow ¾ cup of sugar for every cup of fruit.
Cook for 20–30 minutes to reach setting point.

Three Fruits Marmalade

INGREDIENTS
Orange, 1
Lemon, 1
Grapefruit, 1
Water, 1 litre (4 cups)
Sugar

METHOD

Follow directions on page 58.

Jellies

Jellies make a delicious change from jams. They are actually strained jams without fruit pulp. Jellies are firm and well-flavoured and have a clean, bright colour.

Fruits with high pectin content are the most suitable for jelly making. Fruits with low pectin content can be used if lemon juice or citric acid is added.

For best results from the microwave method, use small quantities of fruit.

Equipment

A jelly bag is required to strain the juices away from the fruit pulp.

Jelly bags can be purchased. They are made of several layers of very fine material, such as cheese cloth, which are attached to a circular frame and stand. They are placed over a basin which catches the strained liquid.

You can make your own jelly bag by tying several layers of cheese cloth to the legs of a chair turned upside down, or you can use a very fine strainer.

Method

1
Wash fruit and chop roughly, leaving pips, cores and skins.

2
Place in a microwave-proof bowl and add water.

3
Cook on HIGH to boiling point (approximately 6–8 minutes) or until soft and pulpy

4
Pour into a clean jelly bag, or a fine strainer, and let stand until juice drips through (for several hours or overnight).
Do not press or squeeze any fruit pulp into juice as this will cloud the jelly.

5
Re-heat juice on HIGH to boiling point. Remove bowl from microwave and stir in required amount of sugar (see page 48) until dissolved. Add lemon juice or citric acid, if required.

6
Return uncovered mixture to microwave and cook on HIGH for approximately 15–20 minutes until setting point has been reached (see page 49).

7
Fill clean, warm sterilised jars to brim with jelly.

8
Fit lids on jars immediately. Do not allow jelly to cool, as warm jelly will create condensation, causing mould.

9
Label and date jars.

10
Store in a cool, dark place.

Apple Jelly

INGREDIENTS
Cooking apples, 5 large
Water, 600 ml (2½ cups)
Sugar

METHOD

Follow directions on page 61.

Blackberry Jelly

INGREDIENTS
Blackberries, 1 kg (2 lbs)
Water, 250 ml (1 cup)
Sugar
Lemon juice, 3 tablespoons
or
Citric acid, 1½ teaspoons

METHOD

Follow directions on page 61.

Blackcurrant Jelly

INGREDIENTS
Blackcurrants, 1 kg (2 lbs)
Water, 250 ml (1 cup)
Sugar
Lemon juice, 2 tablespoons
or
Citric acid, 1 teaspoon

METHOD

Follow directions on page 61.

Crab-apple Jelly

INGREDIENTS
Crab-apples, 1 kg (2 lbs)
Water, 500 ml (2 cups)
Sugar
Lemon juice, 2 tablespoons
or
Citric acid, 1 teaspoon

METHOD

Follow directions on page 61.

Guava Jelly

INGREDIENTS
Guavas, 1 kg (2 lbs)
Water, 600 ml (2½ cups)
Sugar
Lemon juice, 3 tablespoons
or
Citric acid, 1½ teaspoons

METHOD

Follow directions on page 61.

Grape Jelly

INGREDIENTS
Black grapes, 1½ kg (3 lbs)
Water, 125 ml (½ cup)
Sugar
Lemon juice, 3 tablespoons
or
Citric acid, 2 teaspoons

METHOD

Follow directions on page 61.
Note: Allow ¾ cup of sugar for every cup of juice.

Quince Jelly

INGREDIENTS
Quinces, 1 kg (2 lbs)
Water, 600 ml (2½ cups)
Sugar

METHOD

Follow directions on page 61.

Conserves

Conserves are simply jams made with whole fruits, or with large pieces of fruit.

Conserves are usually made from fruits with low pectin content, but high- pectin fruits can also be used. Very little water is added, as this keeps the pectin concentrated, giving the conserve greater setting power.

Method

1
Wash fruit, remove stalks and blemishes, and cut in halves or quarters.

2
Place fruit, water and lemon juice or citric acid in a large microwave-proof bowl and cook on HIGH until soft and pulpy (approximately 3–4 minutes).

3
Measure fruit pulp.

4
Re-heat on HIGH to boiling point.

5
Stir in required amount of sugar (see page 48) until dissolved.

6
Return uncovered mixture to microwave and cook on HIGH for approximately 15–20 minutes until setting point has been reached (see page 49).

7
Fill clean, warm sterilised jars to brim with conserve.

8
Fit lids on jars according to directions on page 6.

9
Label and date jars.

10
Store in a cool, dark place.

Strawberry Conserve

INGREDIENTS
Strawberries, 1 kg (2 lbs)
Water, 125 ml (½ cup)
Lemon juice, 2 tablespoons
or
Citric acid, 1 teaspoon
Sugar

METHOD

Follow directions on page 65.

Fig Conserve

INGREDIENTS
Figs, 1 kg (2 lbs)
Water, 185 ml (¾ cup)
Lemon juice, 2 tablespoons
or
Citric acid, 1 teaspoon
Sugar

METHOD

Follow directions on page 65.

Peach Conserve

INGREDIENTS
Peaches, 1 kg (2 lbs)
Water, 185 ml (¾ cup)
Lemon juice, 2 tablespoons
or
Citric acid, 1 teaspoon
Sugar

METHOD

Follow directions on page 65.

3

Chutneys, Pickles & Relishes

Chutneys, pickles and relishes — all welcome additions to the pantry — are made easily with the microwave method. Fruit and vegetables from a backyard harvest can be transformed into delicious and unusual taste treats, ideal for gifts.

Chutneys are mixtures of fruits and vegetables preserved with vinegar, salt and spices. They can be made at any time of the year with almost any type of fruit and vegetable, and their flavours can be varied according to personal taste. They can be sweet or sour, mild or hot and anything in between.

Pickles are made using vegetables which are soaked in brine for several hours. This process removes excess moisture, keeping the vegetables crisp, and prevents the formation of bacteria.

Equipment

To make chutneys and pickles the following equipment is required:

1 A large, microwave-proof bowl.

2 A large spoon, preferably wooden.

3 Clean jars, free of chips, ridges or other imperfections, and sufficient covers or screw-top lids to fit.

Sterilising the Equipment

To sterilise and warm the jars, follow the instructions on page 47.

Spices

Spices are added to vinegar to improve the flavour. You can use spices according to your taste. Commercially produced spiced vinegar can be used, but a wider variety of flavours is possible if you prepare your own.

Whole spices should be used for pickles, as ground spices will make the vinegar cloudy. However, ground spices should be used for chutneys as they give a stronger flavour. If you use whole spices for chutneys, add more than the amount stated in the recipe and tie them in a muslin bag. The bag can easily be removed before the chutney is bottled.

Brine

For best results use coarse cooking salt, as refined table salt produces a cloudy effect. The ideal solution for soaking vegetables is 125 grams (½ cup) of salt to 2 litres (8 cups) of water. Dissolve the salt in boiling water and cool. Strain the brine before using it, and carefully rinse all traces of it from the vegetables before soaking them in the spiced vinegar.

Vinegar

Use high-quality vinegar in chutneys and pickles. Brown malt vinegar is the usual choice, but wine vinegar can also be used for its special flavour. White malt or cider vinegar are used for pickling light-coloured vegetables.

Spiced Vinegar

1 litre vinegar
1 teaspoon whole cloves
2 teaspoons black peppercorns
2–3 bay leaves
5 cm (2 inches) of cinnamon stick
1 teaspoon mustard seeds

METHOD

Place all ingredients into a microwave proof bowl. Bring spiced vinegar to boiling point approx 5 mins. Remove from oven and allow to cool. Strain and store spiced vinegar in clean bottles ready for use.

Sugar

Chutneys are usually sweetened with white granulated sugar, but brown sugar can be used to make chutneys darker and alter their flavour. Note, however, that a darker chutney can be achieved simply by cooking the mixture for a longer period.

Vacuum Sealing

To vacuum seal the packed jars, follow the instructions on page 49.

Cherry Chutney

INGREDIENTS
Cherries, 1 kg (2 lbs)
or
Preserved cherries and syrup, 700–900 ml
Onions, 2 diced
Green ginger, 1 tablespoon
Brown sugar, 500 g (2 cups)
Raisins, 1 cup
Pinch of nutmeg

Stop Press
375 ml (1½ cups) vinegar to be included in ingredients.

METHOD

1
Remove stems and stones from cherries and wash fruit.

2
Place in a microwave-proof bowl and cook on HIGH until tender (approximately 3–4 minutes).

3
Crush cherries with a potato masher or a fork.

4
Add remaining ingredients to mashed cherries and cook on HIGH until mixture boils. Stir until sugar dissolves.

5
Re-heat on HIGH until mixture thickens.

6
Pack chutney into clean, warm sterilised jars.

7
Fit lids on jars according to directions on page 6.

8
Cook according to table below.

JAR SIZE	OVEN SETTING	COOKING TIME
250–350 ml	medium high	1 mins
400–650 ml	medium high	2 mins
700–900 ml	medium high	3 mins

Note: The cooking times are for 1 jar; add 1 minute for every additional jar.

9
Cool and store according to directions on page 10.

Fruity Banana Chutney

INGREDIENTS
Bananas, 12
Dates, halved and stoned, ¾ cup
Raisins, ½ cup
Sugar, 250 g (1 cup)
Cinnamon, 1 dessertspoon
Malt vinegar, 500 ml (2 cups)
Sultanas, ½ cup
Salt, 1 dessertspoon
Nutmeg, 1 teaspoon
Turmeric, 2 teaspoons

METHOD

1
Peel and slice bananas.

2
Place all ingredients in a microwave-proof bowl and cook
on HIGH until mixture thickens (approximately 15–20
minutes). Stir 2–3 times during cooking.

3
Pack chutney into clean, warm sterilised jars.

4
Fit lids on jars according to directions on page 6.

5
Cook according to table below.

JAR SIZE	OVEN SETTING	COOKING TIME
250–350 ml	*medium high*	*1 mins*
400–650 ml	*medium high*	*2 mins*
700–900 ml	*medium high*	*3 mins*

*Note: The cooking times are for 1 jar; add 1 minute for every
additional jar.*

6
Cool and store according to directions on page 10.

Pickled Beetroot

INGREDIENTS
Beetroot, 6 medium-sized
Water, 250 ml (1 cup)
Dill seeds, 1 teaspoon
Salt, ½ teaspoon
White vinegar, 350 ml (1⅓ cups)
Mustard seeds, 1 tablespoon
Sugar, 250 g (1 cup)

METHOD

1
Place beetroot and water in a microwave-proof bowl.

2
Cook on HIGH until beetroot is tender and skin is loose
(approximately 18–20 minutes).

3
Cool, cut off tops and bottoms, pull away skin, and slice.

4
Place remaining ingredients in a microwave-proof bowl and
cook until mixture boils. Stir until sugar dissolves.

5
Pack beetroot into clean, warm sterilised jars.

6
Fill jars to overflowing with vinegar mixture.

7
Fit lids on jars according to directions on page 6.

8
Cook according to table below.

JAR SIZE	OVEN SETTING	COOKING TIME
250–350 ml	medium high	3 mins
400–650 ml	medium high	4 mins
700–900 ml	medium high	5 mins

*Note: The cooking times are for 1 jar; add 1 minute for every
additional jar.*

9
Cool and store according to directions on page 10.

Pickled Cherries

INGREDIENTS
Cherries, 1 kg (2 lbs)
Water, 250 ml (1 cup)
Dry sherry, 125 ml (½ cup)
Vinegar, 250 ml (1 cup)
Sugar, 250 g (1 cup)
Allspice, ½ teaspoon

METHOD

1
Remove stems and stones from cherries.

2
Place remaining ingredients in a microwave-proof bowl and cook until mixture boils. Stir until sugar dissolves.

3
Pack cherries into clean, warm sterilised jars.

4
Fill jars to overflowing with vinegar mixture.

5
Fit lids on jars according to directions on page 6.

6
Cook according to table below.

JAR SIZE	OVEN SETTING	COOKING TIME
250–350 ml	medium high	2 mins
400–650 ml	medium high	3 mins
700–900 ml	medium high	4 mins

Note: The cooking times are for 1 jar; add 1 minute for every additional jar.

7
Cool and store according to directions on page 10.

Pickled Cucumber

INGREDIENTS
Cucumbers, 4 small, with peel
Cider vinegar, 500 ml (2 cups)
Green capsicums, 2
Sugar, 250 g (1 cup)

METHOD

1
Slice cucumbers into thin circles. Cut capsicums in half,
remove seeds and slice into strips.

2
Dissolve sugar in warmed vinegar.

3
Pack vegetables into clean, warm sterilised jars.

4
Fill jars to overflowing with vinegar mixture.

5
Fit lids on jars according to directions on page 6.

6
Cook according to table below.

JAR SIZE	OVEN SETTING	COOKING TIME
250–350 ml	medium high	3 mins
400–650 ml	medium high	4 mins
700–900 ml	medium high	5 mins

*Note: The cooking times are for 1 jar; add 2 minutes for every
additional jar.*

7
Cool and store according to directions on page 10.

Mango Chutney

INGREDIENTS
Mangoes, 4 medium-sized
Cooking apples, 3
Onions, 350 g (12 oz)
Brown sugar, 500 g (2 cups)
Brown vinegar, 500 ml (2 cups)
Water, 250 ml (1 cup)
Ground ginger, 1 dessertspoon
Allspice, 1 teaspoon
Salt, 1 teaspoon

METHOD

1
Peel mangoes, cut pieces away from stone. Peel, core and chop up apple roughly. Peel and dice onion.

2
Place mango, apple, onion pieces and water in a microwave-proof bowl. Cook on HIGH until tender (approximately 8–10 minutes).

3
Add sugar and stir until dissolved.

4
Stir in remaining ingredients and cook on HIGH until mixture thickens (approximately 20–25 minutes).

5
Pack chutney into clean, warm sterilised jars.

6
Fit lids on jars according to directions on page 6.

7
Cook according to table below.

JAR SIZE	OVEN SETTING	COOKING TIME
250–350 ml	medium high	1 mins
400–650 ml	medium high	2 mins
700–900 ml	medium high	3 mins

Note: The cooking times are for 1 jar; add 1 minute for every additional jar.

8
Cool and store according to directions on page 10.

Mixed Vegetable Pickle

INGREDIENTS
Onions, 500 g (1 lb)
Cucumber, 1
Green or red chillies
Cauliflower, 500 g (1 lb)
French beans, 500 g (1 lb)
Spiced vinegar, 900 g (3¾ cups)
Brine

METHOD

1
Peel onions and cut in half. Cut cucumber into large cubes and break cauliflower into small pieces. Trim beans to 5 cm (2½ inch) lengths.

2
Soak vegetables in brine for 24 hours.

3
Drain, rinse and pack vegetables into clean, warm sterilised jars.

4
Add a chilli to each jar.

5
Fill jars to overflowing with spiced vinegar.

6
Fit lids on jars according to directions on page 6.

7
Cook according to table below.

JAR SIZE	OVEN SETTING	COOKING TIME
250–350 ml	*medium high*	*3 mins*
400–650 ml	*medium high*	*4 mins*
700–900 ml	*medium high*	*5 mins*

Note: The cooking times are for 1 jar; add 2 minutes for every additional jar.

8
Cool and store according to directions on page 10.

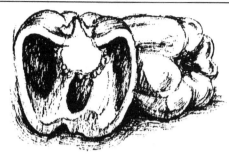

Mustard Pickles

INGREDIENTS

Onions, small pickling size, 6–8
Zucchini (courgettes), 2
Red pepper, 1
Cauliflower, 1 small
Plain flour, 90 g (¾ cup)
Turmeric, 1 teaspoon
French beans, 10–12
Sugar, 175 g (¾ cup)
Dry mustard, 3 tablespoons
Malt vinegar, 1 litre (4 cups)

METHOD

1
Peel onions and leave whole. Slice zucchini into rings and break cauliflower into small pieces. Cut beans in half.

2
Soak vegetables in brine for 24 hours.

3
Mix flour, sugar, mustard and turmeric with a little vinegar.

4
Cook remaining vinegar on HIGH to boiling point.

5
Stir in blended flour mixture, return to microwave, and cook on HIGH until mixture thickens (approximately 3–4 minutes).

6
Drain and rinse vegetables, add to thickened sauce and cook on HIGH for 2–3 minutes.

7
Remove vegetables from sauce and pack into clean, warm sterilised jars.

8
Fill jars to brim with sauce.

9
Fit lids on jars according to directions on page 6.

10
Cook according to table below.

JAR SIZE	OVEN SETTING	COOKING TIME
250–350 ml	medium high	1 mins
400–650 ml	medium high	2 mins
700–900 ml	medium high	3 mins

Note: The cooking times are for 1 jar; add 1 minute for every additional jar.

11
Cool and store according to directions on page 10.

Black or Green Olives

INGREDIENTS
Black or green olives
Salt
Olive oil

METHOD

1
Prick each olive all over with a needle or a small skewer.

2
Put olives in a plastic colander or a strainer and place over a basin. Sprinkle heavily with salt and toss until all olives are covered.

3
Set aside until olives lose their bitterness (approximately 3 days), tossing 2–3 times each day.

4
Add a little more salt to replace drained salt, and pack olives into clean, warm sterilised jars.

5
Fill jars to brim with olive oil.

6
Fit lids on jars according to directions on page 6.

7
Cool and store according to directions on page 10.

Honey & Onion Slices

INGREDIENTS
Onions
Honey, 4 tablespoons
Vinegar, 250 ml (1 cup)

METHOD

1
Peel and slice enough onions to fill a jar.

2
Pack onions into clean, warm sterilised jar.

3
Stir honey into vinegar, and fill jar to brim.

4
Fit lid on jar according to directions on page 6.

5
Cook according to table below.

JAR SIZE	OVEN SETTING	COOKING TIME
250–350 ml	*medium high*	*3 mins*
400–650 ml	*medium high*	*4 mins*
700–900 ml	*medium high*	*5 mins*

Note: The cooking times are for 1 jar; add 1 minute for every additional jar.

6
Cool and store according to directions on page 10.

Pickled Onions

INGREDIENTS
Onions, small pickling size, 500 g (1 lb)
Spiced vinegar, 900 g (3¾ cups)
Brine

METHOD

1
Peel onions and soak in brine for 24 hours.
3
Drain, rinse and pack onions into clean, warm sterilised jars.
4
Fill jars to overflowing with spiced vinegar.
5
Fit lids on jars according to directions on page 6.
6
Cook according to table below.

JAR SIZE	OVEN SETTING	COOKING TIME
250–350 ml	*medium high*	*3 mins*
400–650 ml	*medium high*	*4 mins*
700–900 ml	*medium high*	*5 mins*

Note: The cooking times are for 1 jar; add 2 minutes for every additional jar.

7
Cool and store according to directions on page 10.

Peach Chutney

INGREDIENTS
Yellow cooking peaches, 2 kg (4 lbs)
or
Preserved peaches and syrup, 2 × 700–900 ml jars
Brown sugar, 500 g (2 cups)
Cayenne pepper, ½ teaspoon
Vinegar, 1 litre (4 cups)
Green ginger, 90 g (3 oz)
Crushed garlic, 1 tablespoon
Raisins, 1 cup

METHOD

1

Peel peaches with a stainless steel knife or a peeling utensil, or immerse in boiling water for 2 minutes then pull away skin.

2

Slice peaches and place in a microwave-proof bowl. Cook on HIGH for 8–10 minutes.

3

Add sugar and stir until dissolved.

4

Re-heat on HIGH until mixture is consistency of jam (approximately 15–18 minutes) and cool.

5

Chop ginger and raisins finely.

6

Add all ingredients to peaches and cook on HIGH for 8–10 minutes.

7

Pack chutney into clean, warm sterilised jars.

8

Fit lids on jars according to directions on page 6.

9

Cook according to table below.

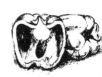

JAR SIZE	OVEN SETTING	COOKING TIME
250–350 ml	medium high	1 mins
400–650 ml	medium high	2 mins
700–900 ml	medium high	3 mins

Note: The cooking times are for 1 jar; add 1 minute for every additional jar.

10
Cool and store according to directions on page 10.

Plum Chutney

INGREDIENTS
Dark red or blue plums, 1 kg (2 lbs)
Cooking apples, 750 g (1½ lbs)
Brown vinegar, 375 ml (1½ cups)
Salt, 1 teaspoon
Onions 250 g (½ lb)
Brown sugar, 250 g (½ lb)
Water, 125 ml (½ cup)
Whole cloves, 1 teaspoon
Black peppercorns, 1 teaspoon
Allspice, 1 teaspoon

METHOD

1
Wash plums, halve and remove stones. Peel and core apples, then chop roughly. Peel and dice onions.

2
Place in a microwave-proof bowl with water and cook on HIGH until tender (approximately 8–10 minutes).

3
Tie spices in a muslin bag and place in a microwave-proof bowl with sugar and vinegar. Cook on HIGH until liquid boils.

4
Stir until sugar dissolves.

5
Re-heat on HIGH and boil for 2–3 minutes. Remove muslin bag.

6
Pour spiced vinegar into fruit and vegetable mixture.

7
Cook on HIGH until mixture thickens (approximately 15–18 minutes).

8
Pack chutney into clean, warm sterilised jars.

9
Fit lids on jars according to directions on page 6.

10
Cook according to table below.

JAR SIZE	OVEN SETTING	COOKING TIME
250–350 ml	medium high	1 mins
400–650 ml	medium high	2 mins
700–900 ml	medium high	3 mins

Note: The cooking times are for 1 jar; add 1 minute for every additional jar.

11
Cool and store according to directions on page 10.

Green Tomato Chutney

INGREDIENTS
Green tomatoes, 500 g (1 lb)
Cooking apple, 1 large
Garlic, 1 clove, crushed
Sugar, 125 g (½ cup)
Ground ginger, 1 teaspoon
Onions, 2 medium-sized
Green capsicum, 1
Green chillies, 3
Malt vinegar, 125 ml (½ cup)
Salt, ½ teaspoon

METHOD

1
Coarsely chop tomatoes, onions and apples.
Dice capsicum, removing stem, seeds and white pith.
Slit open chillies, remove seeds and chop flesh finely.

2
Place all ingredients in a microwave-proof bowl, cover with
a loose-fitting lid, or pierced plastic wrap (steam needs to
escape during cooking), and cook on HIGH until mixture
thickens (approximately 15–20 minutes).

3
Pack chutney into clean, warm sterilised jars.

4
Fit lids on jars according to directions on page 6.

5
Cook according to table below.

JAR SIZE	*OVEN SETTING*	*COOKING TIME*
250–350 ml	*medium high*	*1 mins*
400–650 ml	*medium high*	*2 mins*
700–900 ml	*medium high*	*3 mins*

*Note: The cooking times are for 1 jar; add 1 minute for every
additional jar.*

6
Cool and store according to directions on page 10.

Spicy Red Tomatoes

INGREDIENTS
Ripe tomatoes, 2.5 kg (5 lbs)
Brown sugar, 1 kg (2 lbs)
Vinegar, 750 ml (3 cups)
Mixed spice, 1 tablespoon
Ground cinnamon, 1 tablespoon
Ground cloves, 1 teaspoon

METHOD

1
Immerse tomatoes in boiling water for 2–3 minutes, then peel off skins.

2
Pack tomatoes into clean, warm sterilised jars.

3
Place sugar, vinegar and spices in a microwave-proof bowl and cook until mixture thickens to the consistency of cream (approximately 8–10 minutes).

4
Fill jars to brim with mixture.

5
Fit lids on jars according to directions on page 6.

6
Cook according to table below.

JAR SIZE	OVEN SETTING	COOKING TIME
250–350 ml	medium high	2 mins
400–650 ml	medium high	3 mins
700–900 ml	medium high	4 mins

Note: The cooking times are for 1 jar; add 1 minute for every additional jar.

7
Cool and store according to directions on page 10.

Index

86